# Contents

The story in this book is a real story and takes place in Egypt. Egypt is a very hot country. Perhaps you know someone who has been there.

This is Cairo. It is the biggest city in Egypt. Is it like a city you know? What looks different? What looks the same?

Outside Cairo you come to a sandy desert where there is a famous statue called the Sphinx. It is half human and half lion.

The building behind the Sphinx is a pyramid. You can see how big it is if you look at the people standing at the bottom.

The people looking at the Sphinx and the pyramid are tourists. They are looking at two of the oldest buildings in the world. The people who built them lived in Egypt more than four thousand years ago.

People travel from all over the world to find out about the Egyptian people of **ancient times**.
Most people who go to Egypt from Britain go by air. It takes about five hours.

At the time of our story aeroplanes were very small and did not fly very far, so people had to go from Britain to Egypt by ship. It took two weeks.

**Ancient times**

A very long time ago indeed.

# The people in the story

In this story you will read about some real people and what happened to them.
The people were:

**Howard Carter**
He was an **archaeologist** from Britain working in Egypt.

**Lord Carnarvon** and **Lady Evelyn Herbert**
They were rich people from Britain who were interested in Ancient Egypt. Lord Carnarvon gave the money to pay the bills for Howard Carter's work in Egypt.

**Archaeologist**

Someone who finds out about the past from clues buried under the ground.

### The workers
We do not know their names. They were Egyptian people who helped the archaeologists. Their job was to dig in the desert sand and carry it away in baskets. They had to dig carefully, in case they broke something buried in the sand.

### A waterboy
We do not know his name. His job was to take water to the workers. Everyone got very thirsty working in the hot desert.

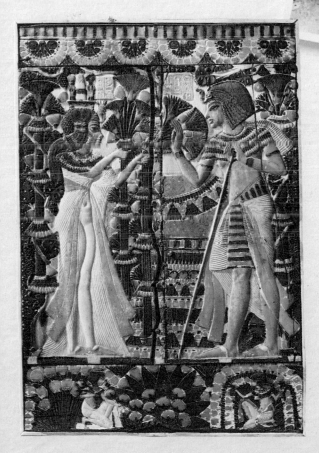

### King Tutankhamun and Queen Ankesenanum
Tutankhamun was a ruler, or **pharaoh**, of Egypt in ancient times. He died when he was only eighteen. He and Ankesenanum had just got married. The archaeologists were trying to find the place where his body had been buried.

**Pharaoh**

The title given to the kings of ancient Egypt.

The events of this story took place over sixty years ago in 1922, but what Howard Carter and his helpers found took them thousands of years back in history.

It all happened here at a place in Egypt called the Valley of the Kings. This photograph shows the valley just as it was when Carter arrived. Colour film had not been invented then. That is why some of the photographs in this book are in black and white.

The people of ancient Egypt had buried some of their greatest kings, called pharaohs, in this valley. You can see the entrance to one of the graves in the picture.

Archaeologists found the graves in the twentieth century. By 1922 they thought they had found them all. But Howard Carter worked out that there was still one left — the grave of Tutankhamun.

# What did Howard Carter hope to find?

## What was so interesting about a grave?

The Egyptians believed that when they died they would make a journey to another world where they would lead a new life. They would need all the things they had used when they were alive, so their families put these things into the grave.

The Egyptians buried their pharaohs in a special sort of grave. It was a big underground room called a tomb.

Howard Carter hoped to find a tomb full of treasure, because the pharaohs were very rich.

He hoped to find something else too. He was looking for the **mummy** of the dead king. He hoped that the king would look just as he did on the day he died.

### What is a mummy?

The Egyptians believed dead bodies must not be allowed to rot, so they used special ointments and wax to preserve them.

The Arabs call a preserved body a 'mumiya' and we have turned this word into 'mummy'.

Here is the grave of an Egyptian man who died even earlier than Tutankhamun. His family buried him in a hole in the sand.
Find the pots. They were to hold his things.

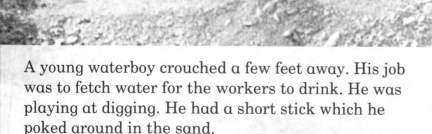

It was early morning on the third of November 1922 in a hot and dusty desert valley in Egypt. Some Egyptian workers were searching for something by carefully digging away sand and stones. They were working for Howard Carter. But they worked half-heartedly, without much hope.

A young waterboy crouched a few feet away. His job was to fetch water for the workers to drink. He was playing at digging. He had a short stick which he poked around in the sand.

Suddenly he hit a hard surface. He dug furiously and in a few moments he had uncovered a stone step.

He stared at it. Then he quickly covered it over again so that the others couldn't see it and ran to tell Carter what he had found.

Quickly Carter ordered the workers to clear away the sand around the waterboy's step. Gradually they uncovered twelve more.

Then they found the top part of a door made of brick and plaster. Carter bent down to look. He saw this stamped onto the plaster.

It showed a wild dog. Underneath the dog were nine prisoners tied up with rope.

Carter was excited. He knew that in ancient times the **priests** of the royal burial ground used to stamp this picture on the door of a royal tomb when they closed it for the last time.

This meant that the door would lead to the tomb of a very important person.

But whose tomb? There were no clues.

At sunset Carter ordered the workers to cover the steps over again. He didn't want anyone else to find the tomb. That night he sent a telegram to his friend Lord Carnarvon in Scotland, asking him to come at once.

Lord Carnarvon was a rich man who was interested in Ancient Egypt. Five years before, he had agreed to pay the bills for Howard Carter's search for Tutankhamun's tomb. This discovery sounded too good to be true. Would it be a false alarm?

Carnarvon and his daughter, Lady Evelyn, arrived in Egypt two weeks later. They went to a town called Luxor, not far from the Valley of the Kings. Howard Carter and the Egyptian governor of the area met them there.

AT LAST HAVE MADE WONDERFUL DISCOVERY IN THE VALLEY.
A MAGNIFICENT TOMB WITH SEALS INTACT. RECOVERED SAME
FOR YOUR ARRIVAL. CONGRATULATIONS.
H. CARTER.

### 'Seals Intact'

The picture the priests had stamped on the door of the tomb was called a **seal** because it was used to seal up the door. **Intact** means unbroken. If the seals were unbroken it meant that no one had been in there since the priests had left.

Then they made their way up into the hills to the Valley of the Kings to see the tomb.

The next day Carter asked the workers
to break down the door. They found a
passage blocked by stones and rubble.
Slowly they cleared them away.

Then they found a second door.

Carter took an iron bar and made a
tiny hole in the top left–hand corner.
The bar passed through. That meant
that the passage behind was clear.
Carter lit a candle.
He put the flame up to the
hole to test for dangerous
gases. He widened the
hole a little and looked in.

At first he saw nothing.
Hot air escaping through
the hole made the candle
flame flicker. Then his
eyes adjusted. He saw
strange animals, statues
and gold, everywhere the
glint of gold. "Can you see
anything?" Carnarvon asked.
"Yes," Carter said, "Wonderful things!"

This photograph was taken after Carter
and Carnarvon had opened the tomb.

They put a steel gate over the entrance
to protect the treasures inside.

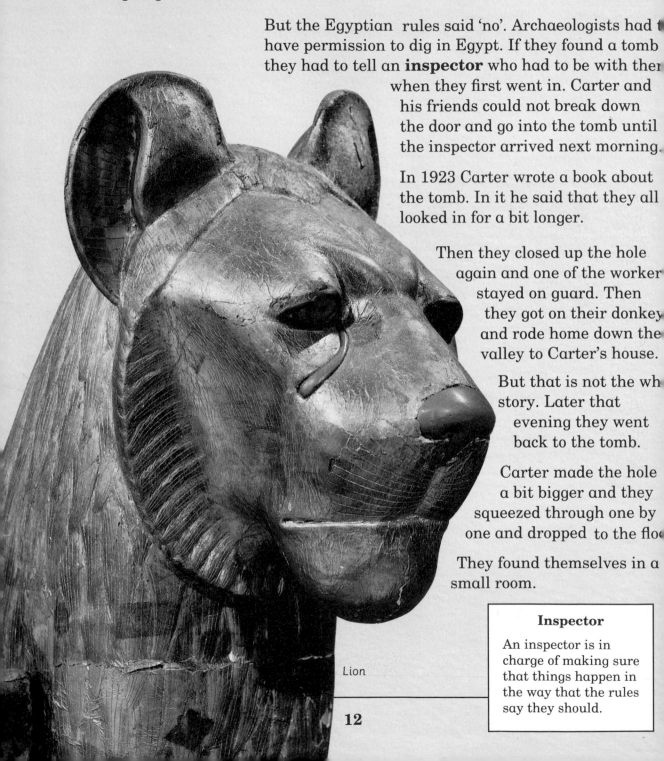

Carter made the hole big enough for them to get their heads in and flash a torch round. They desperately wanted to go right in and have a closer look.

But the Egyptian rules said 'no'. Archaeologists had to have permission to dig in Egypt. If they found a tomb they had to tell an **inspector** who had to be with them when they first went in. Carter and his friends could not break down the door and go into the tomb until the inspector arrived next morning.

In 1923 Carter wrote a book about the tomb. In it he said that they all looked in for a bit longer.

Then they closed up the hole again and one of the workers stayed on guard. Then they got on their donkeys and rode home down the valley to Carter's house.

But that is not the whole story. Later that evening they went back to the tomb.

Carter made the hole a bit bigger and they squeezed through one by one and dropped to the floor.

They found themselves in a small room.

Lion

12

### Inspector

An inspector is in charge of making sure that things happen in the way that the rules say they should.

Over three thousand years had passed since the room had been sealed up, but it seemed like yesterday. A bunch of flowers still with its petals and leaves lay by the doorway. They saw a fingerprint that had been left on the painted surface of an oil lamp. The smell of perfumes was still in the air.

Along the wall opposite the door were three golden beds. They were carved into the shape of animals. There was a lion, a cow and a typhon. A typhon was part hippopotamus and part crocodile. The animals' eyes seemed to blink in the torchlight.

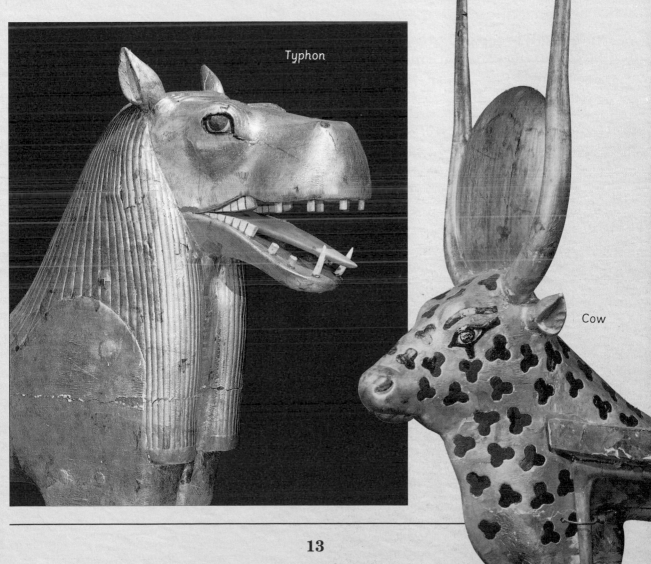

Typhon

Cow

Then they found a
beautiful golden throne
with the figures of
Tutankhamun and Queen
Ankesenanum shown on
the back.

Only one thing worried
Carter: if this was
Tukankhamun's tomb, where was the
King's dead body? He found another
small room full of treasure but there was
no coffin.

On the wall to the right they saw two
life size statues of King Tutankhamun.
The statues stood opposite each other,
as if on guard.

Then he realised that the two statues of the King stood
either side of a sealed-up entrance in the
north wall.

In his book Carter says he waited over two months for the official opening before he went through this entrance. But Lady Evelyn told Carnarvon's half-brother a secret which he wrote in his diary. The secret was that that night they made a small hole in the wall near the floor and went through.

When they stood up on the other side they knew that they had reached the tomb itself. Opposite them stood a huge wooden case covered in gold. Carter was sure that the King's coffin lay behind its doors.

Then Carter saw an opening to yet another room.
He flashed his light inside and there, guarding the
entrance, was a large statue of a wild dog carved in
black wood. It lay on top of a tall box with its head
up, watchful like a guard dog.

It was time to leave. As they went back into the first
room, Carter blocked up the wall again and covered
the spot with a basket.

In the morning the inspector arrived and they took down the door to the first room. They had to pretend they had not been in before.

It was full of beautiful things like this vase and this box.

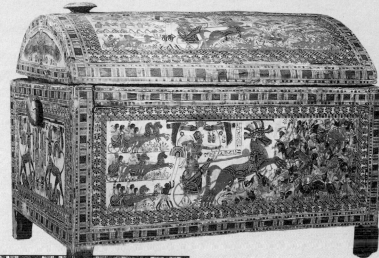

The painting on the side shows the Pharaoh Tutankhamun in his chariot, scattering the enemies of Egypt.

There were so many important objects in the tomb that Carter had to ask for a team of people to help him. It took three years to deal with them all.

They took a photograph of each object. They made a drawing on a small card and wrote a description. Then they drew a plan to show where it lay in the tomb.

They tried to put back together things that had broken or fallen to bits because they were so old.

Then they had to wrap everything up and put it all into cases to go to Cairo. Here is Howard Carter wrapping up one of the statues. Over two miles of bandages were used in one year.

At last they were ready to open the doors of the big wooden box covered in gold. It was a kind of house for the king's coffin.

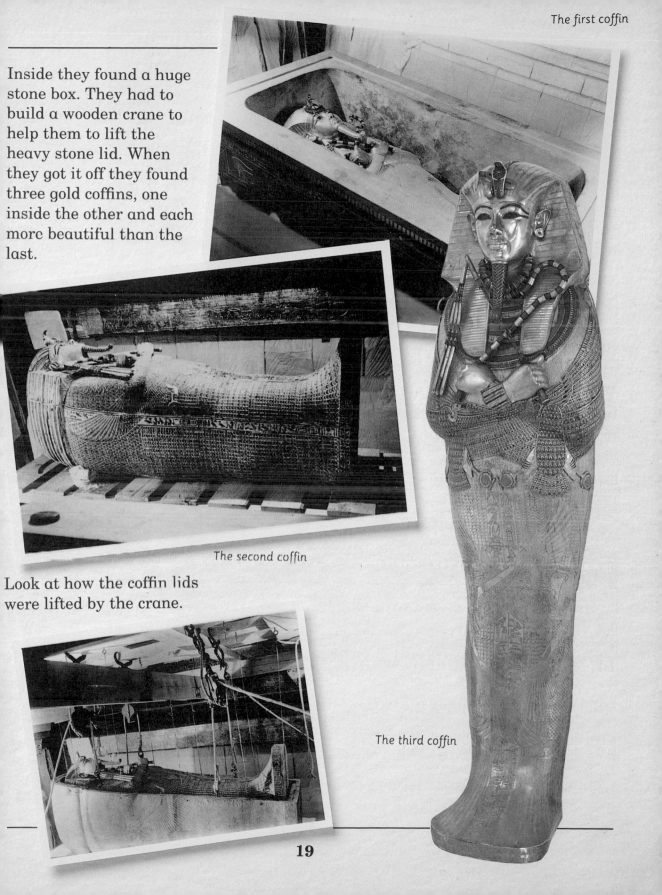

Inside they found a huge stone box. They had to build a wooden crane to help them to lift the heavy stone lid. When they got it off they found three gold coffins, one inside the other and each more beautiful than the last.

The second coffin

Look at how the coffin lids were lifted by the crane.

The third coffin

19

Inside the third coffin lay the bandaged mummy.

This life-size gold mask of the king covered its face.
It is made of solid gold and blue glass.

What do you think Carter felt like as he looked at this
wonderful portrait of the handsome young king?

The big moment had come. It was time to cut away the bandages round the mummy.

Doctors and scientists came from Cairo to help. On the eleventh of November 1925 they made the first cut with a surgeon's knife.

They found thirteen layers of bandages. Hidden among them were one hundred and forty pieces of jewellery.

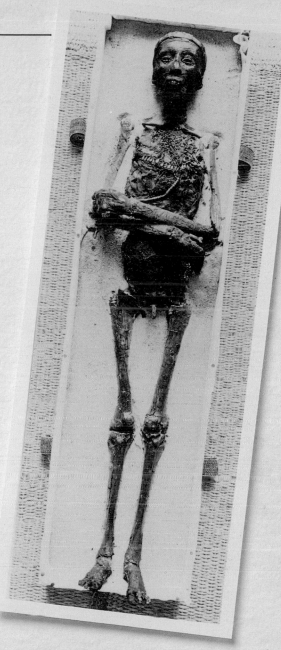

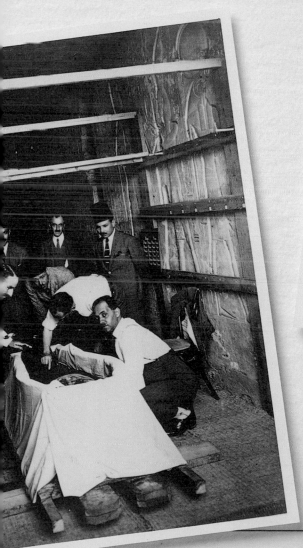

In the end they came to the body itself. With fine, soft brushes Howard Carter moved the last pieces of cloth from the face.

At last, after years of detective work, Howard Carter had come face to face with the young Pharaoh Tutankhamun.

# A quarrel

Lord Carnarvon never saw the mummy of the dead king. He became ill and died in 1923, the year after Howard Carter found the tomb. Before he died, Carnarvon quarrelled with the Egyptians.

The trouble began when newspaper reporters arrived from all over the world to write about the amazing discoveries in the tomb. Howard Carter said they were getting in his way and holding up the work.

What was Carnarvon to do? He decided to sell the right to go into the tomb to just one newspaper. He chose *The Times* of London.

The Egyptians were furious. They said that the tomb was in their country and Carnarvon was wrong to choose a foreign newspaper. Anyway, they said, he had no right to make money out of the tomb by selling information.

Then the Egyptians asked if some of their archaeologists could go into the tomb to watch the work. Carter said 'no' because they would get in the way. He said the crowds of tourists who kept coming to watch were bad enough. Do you think he was right?

COUVERTE ARCHÉOLOGIQUE
TOMBEAU
hamen, roi d'Egypte
GYPTIAN
ASURE.

FIND AT

ROYAL TOMB AN
TREASURES

MISSED IN 1911 BY
YARDS.

KING TUTANKHA!

THE RESTORER OF "O

DE

WIDESPREAD REGRET.

MESSAGE FROM KING
GEORGE.

DEATH OF LO
CARNARVO

RSDAY, APRIL 5.

of Carnarvon Dies o

ct Bite Near Pharao

mb That He Discove

LORD CARNARVON

SUDDEN COT

PEAC

Editoria

When Lord Carnarvon died, things got
worse. Howard Carter said that he was
in charge of the way things were done
at the tomb. The Egyptians said that he
had to do what they wanted.

In the end the Egyptian Prime Minister
wrote to Howard Carter. He said, "I
must remind you that the tomb is not
your property."

Carter became so angry that he and his
helpers locked the tomb and went away
with the keys, saying they would not go
on with the work.

They had just lifted the big stone lid off
the box with the gold coffins inside.
They left the lid swinging on the end of
ropes. If the ropes were to break, the lid
would fall and smash the coffins to
pieces.

The Egyptians said this showed that
Howard Carter did not really care
about archaeology. They had to break
the lock on the tomb and go in and
lower the stone lid.

This quarrel went on for nearly a year.
In the end Carter agreed to do what the
Egyptians wanted.

The Egyptian Prime Minister, Zaghlul Pasha

It took Howard Carter until 1932 to finish clearing all the things from the tomb. After that he lived in England. He visited Egypt several times, but he did no more digging there. He died in 1939. Nearly everything from the tomb was taken to the Egyptian Museum in Cairo where you can still see it today.

This little statue is about fifteen centimetres high. It came from the tomb but you can't see it in the Egyptian Museum. It is in a museum in Paris.

There were four hundred and fourteen statues like this in the tomb and Howard Carter made notes on four hundred and thirteen of them. This is the one that he missed. Somebody must have taken it away without permission before Carter had finished making his notes.